Thomas Brodhead Van Buren

Analysis of the Evidence and Reports

On the Vienna Scandal

Thomas Brodhead Van Buren

Analysis of the Evidence and Reports
On the Vienna Scandal

ISBN/EAN: 9783337404406

Printed in Europe, USA, Canada, Australia, Japan

Cover: Foto ©ninafisch / pixelio.de

More available books at **www.hansebooks.com**

ANALYSIS

—OF THE—

EVIDENCE AND REPORTS,

—ON THE—

Vienna Scandal

LETTER FROM

General T. B. Van Buren,

LATE CHIEF COMMISSIONER

—TO THE—

SECRETARY OF STATE.

To the Honorable Hamilton Fish,

Secretary of State.

Sir:—Since my return to the country a few weeks ago, I have read, for the first time, what purports to be the evidence taken before Messrs. Jay and McElrath, in the city of Vienna, Austria, in relation to the acts and doings of the U. S. Commission to the International Exhibition in that city; and the elaborate libel accompanying that evidence, signed by them, which they endeavor to dignify by the title of a "report."

This evidence and report, together with a portion of the correspondence between the Honorable Secretary of State and myself, are embraced in a massive volume in book form, prepared at the Department of State.

The title page of this volume proclaims it to contain the "Charges against General T. B. Van Buren and the replies thereto."

As no "charges" have ever been presented to me, I have been afforded no opportunity of reply, and I have searched through three hundred pages of this book, in vain, to ascertain the charges, unless they are to be found in the telegrams of Mr. Jay or extracted from the verbiage of the report.

In a letter from you, dated the 12th of September, 1873, occurs the following language: "*It certainly was not the Department of State nor the Government which assigned any criminality or improper conduct, or anything but 'irregularities' as the cause of suspension.*" And again—"*The Government assigned no grounds for the suspension which should necessarily overwhelm one with mortification and distress. If newspapers assigned any such grounds, the Government was not responsible therefor.*" I am obliged to confess my ignorance of what misdemeanors may be included under the comprehensive term "irregularities"—but am warranted in concluding, from your language just quoted, that "nothing criminal or improper" is embraced within its meaning—and also that whatever acts or omissions it implies must have existed prior to the date of my suspension. Again, these "irregularities," whatever they are, must have been entirely unknown to the Government prior to my departure for Europe, and must have been, it is fair to assume, of a most serious character to have induced the suspension of the American Commission at Vienna, a few days before the opening of the Exhibition. Permit me to say I find no such charges in the volume before me, and am at as much loss to-day, as I was at the time of my removal, to know of what I am accused. One thing, however, I think must be apparent to the most casual reader of these pages, and that is the intense, bitter, personal, malignant hostility of the Honorable John Jay to the Commission—and his persistent and successful efforts to destroy it at whatever cost to the reputation of his Government and at whatever peril to the Exhibition.

I would that his letters to the Department of State during the winter and spring of 1872-3 might have been included in this volume, affording additional evidence, as they do, of his malice towards the Commission and of his designs to embarass and defeat its labors. Of this interference on the part of Mr. Jay I frequently expressed my opinion, as reference to my letters will show, and finally announced to you that if it could not be prevented I preferred to surrender my commission.

Within a few weeks after my appointment I received warning of this disposition of Mr. Jay's. And these warnings were repeated in various quarters, during the progress of my work, and even on my journey to Vienna. But conscious as I was of having performed my duty faithfully and knowing too that the Honorable Secretary of State was aware, to some extent, of this hostility on Mr. Jay's part, I paid no further heed to this warning, relying as I did upon the full protection of my Government. Mr. Jay, however, was confident in his power of evil, and in that confidence boasted of his intent to destroy my Commission long before I reached Vienna, if I am to believe the reports of those who claim to have received such information. While I remained in the country his efforts in this connection were fruitless, but as soon as my departure was known, he made such use of the telegraphic cable as to prove that his boasts were not vain.

I can well appreciate the harshness and power of these telegrams. As I read them now in the pages before me, I can understand how they affected the Honorable Secretary of State, who felt called upon to act upon the positive statements of the Government's accredited minister; but I suggest that had these messages been communicated to me and my reply requested I could have given to the Government such explanations, backed by incontestable evidence, that the great scandal which followed, and the public disgrace in a foreign land, of officers bearing U. S. Commissions, must have been averted.

Assassination has never, under any circumstances, been considered a manly act, but poisoning the guest at one's table, or using the poinard at one's fireside, has always been held the resort of the most despicable cowardice and villainy. On the 20th of April, in reply to a letter from the Secretary of State, Mr. Jay wrote (p. 115): "I note the hope which you express that 'there may be an entire and cordial understanding between myself and the Commissioner,' and beg to say that I will use *my* best endeavors to accomplish your wishes in this respect." And on the 16th he added (p. 119): "My relations with General Van Buren are friendly, and he and his wife dine with me to-morrow." This is true! We did dine at his table; but little did I suspect, while enjoying his hospitalities, that the guests about that table had been confidentially informed that I was to be removed in disgrace, and that the same information was in possession of restaurant keepers and others in Vienna. That such was the fact, however, I have been again and again assured.

The motive of Mr. Jay in his crusade against my commission it is scarcely necessary here to analyze. But if any unpredjudiced man can gather from a perusal of this record, as made up by himself, that it was to guard the reputation and honor of his country, I shall make no effort to convince that man to the contrary. The fact remains that his designs were successful, and the result of his efforts to justify his acts is seen in the evidence and reports he has filed with the Department.

"THE SPECIAL COMMISSION."

I have once before protested against the character of the tribunal established upon the recommendation of Mr. Jay, to carry out his purposes, and I now desire to renew that protest in the most earnest terms. Mr. Jay, my accuser and foe, whose persistent endeavors to destroy my commission were, even at that time, a public scandal, was made chief judge and manager, and his assistant on the bench was selected from my own appointees, who was thus made judge over his chief, his fellow Commissioners and himself. Having theretofore held a federal office in New York City, he was removed by the President with charges standing against him for malfeasance in office, which charges are still unexplained, and which were unknown to me at the time of his appointment. Both on this account and because he was one of the Assistant Commissioners which the tribunal was authorized to suspend, I submit he was entirely disqualified from acting as a member of it. No right-minded men, situated as were Messrs. Jay and McElrath, could have consented to serve on the examining commission. They were estopped by their positions and previous acts, and could never be considered as fair or impartial judges. But not only did Mr. McElrath sit as examiner and judge, but he became a swift witness, detailing conversations brought about by himself, and the gossip of the streets and hotels. Going about from General Meyer to myself, claiming to be the especial friend of each, he faithfully carried out the tactics of his principal, and commended himself to the good graces of that high-minded official.

I protest also that the proceedings of that tribunal, as conducted by Messrs. Jay and McElrath, and which I believe to have been contrary to the wishes and intent of the Government, were without warrant in the Consti-tution, laws or precedents of our country, and were sub-versive of the rights of citizens.

In the first place, their examinations were secret. Each witness was examined by himself, without the presence of any parties except the examiners and their clerk. Mr. Jay was understood to be the manager of the American Department of the Exhibition, and held in his hand the rights of exhibitors and the reputation and official life of the Commissioners—while Mr. McElrath was but his agent and echo.

I was not permitted to be present at any of the exam-inations, or to cross-examine a single witness, although I demanded such right. In some cases, as I am in-formed, the evidence was not fully or correctly taken.

One striking instance of this omission occurs in my own testimony. During the course of my examination, I was handed a list of the associate Commissioners, and asked by Mr. Jay to indicate those of *foreign birth*.

I pointed out the names of some I supposed to be adopted citizens, but replied that I had not asked a man's birth-place, in selecting my assistants ; that I thought if that question was ignored in raising soldiers for our defense, it could be dispensed with in the choice of commissioners at an exhibition. He asked me a number of questions in reference to this matter, and yet not one word of it all appears in the reported testimony.

Mr. Jay's hostility to *untitled foreigners* was currently

reported at Vienna; but he seems to have thought it imprudent to permit any indications of such disposition on his part to appear in a report to his Government, and which might be made known to the people of our country.

The value of cross-examination has been too often demonstrated, and the right too well established to need discussion here. Had that right been accorded in this instance, I think no comments would have been necessary upon the result. But not only was I not permitted to examine or cross-examine witnesses, but I was denied the right to hear the evidence after it was taken. The great mass of testimony I have never seen or heard until I read it in the book before me. Upon my demand, Mr. Jay has reluctantly, now and then, stated what he called " the material portions of the evidence of a witness;" but, as I read the testimony now, I find that much he has deemed material enough to form the basis of the most virulent portions of his report was kept concealed from me.

GENERAL MAYER.

It is hardly necessary to say that I had formed a sincere attachment for General Mayer. His labors as Commissioner had been performed under my eye. Early and late, for many months, he toiled in the office of the Commission, doing an amount of patient and severe work that won for him my warm approval and regard. I found him an amiable and accomplished man, meeting the constant vexations of his position with patience and courtesy, and apparently doing all it was in his power to do for the success of the Exhibition. Mr. Jay cannot understand how these qualities could have thus commended this man to me. In his opinion, such regard as I manifested for him was the proof of some guilty commerce between us. Entertaining this regard, and feeling the most perfect confidence in Mayer's integrity, I scorned the temptation held out to me by Mr. McElrath, to turn my back upon him when attacked in Vienna. I stood by him, because I believed him innocent of wrong, and that he was to be made the victim of a base conspiracy.

It may be considered by Messrs. Jay and McElrath a praiseworthy virtue to desert a man under such circumstances. To me, it was simple duty to stand by him until convicted of wrong. This sealed my condemnation and I was removed.

Every effort, from that time forth, on the part of Messrs. Jay and McElrath, their spies and informers, was to justify or excuse this removal. The "investigation" (a simple reading of the evidence will show) was not to ascertain the truth, but to get hold of something, however trivial or from whatever source, against me. To that end, witnesses were sought for and plied with innumerable questions, clearly indicating the desires of their examiners. Mayer has asserted over and over again, that they intimated advantages to him if he would only testify something to my injury, and that his invariable reply was that "he had nothing but good to say of me." True, he quibbles about this, when called before them in my absence, still entertaining the hope that those august and powerful gentlemen would modify his sentence, but he repeats it in his letter to the President, which I have read, for the first time, since my return, in these words : "Yes, sir ; I solemnly swear that inducements have been held out to me that, if I would testify against General Van Buren, I should be vindicated and, no doubt, reinstated."

They succeeded in obtaining some general statements from him. "He had acted under his superior;" "General Van Buren approved his acts;" "General Van Buren knew of his obtaining the second thousand dollars," etc. Up to this time nothing immoral had appeared in his acts. Now, under the manipulation of this secret council and its agents, he partially sold himself to their base uses, and falsely endeavored to cast wrong upon me.

Only a portion of his testimony was even stated to me. On his examination, on the 22d of April, he produced and spread upon the record a letter addressed to me on the 16th, but which I did not receive until some time afterwards, and which was evidently written for the purpose of making it testimony. In a personal interview, after its receipt, he so explained it away and apologized for it that no reply was necessary. A subsequent one, however, of a somewhat similar character, received the answer it deserved. Had I known that either of his letters was made a part of the evidence, I should have insisted upon their receiving my reply;—and I now insert extracts from it, that the intention of Messrs. Jay and McElrath, in having it stand as an uncontradicted accusation on the part of Mayer, may be frustrated.

EXTRACTS FROM MY LETTER TO MAYER.

Could I be surprised at anything nowadays, I should express my profound astonishment at the contents of your letter, in which you refuse to deliver to me the accounts and monies of the Commission, and accuse me of various offences.

The friendship and confidence you have received from me have been of no ordinary character. * * * I have steadily maintained this attachment, as no one knows better than yourself, under the most trying circumstances. Your industry, devotion to your duties and professed regard for me were the basis of my trust. * * I was fully persuaded you were true, honest and upright. * * When trouble came to you in London, I sympathized with you most deeply, and expressed my hope and belief that you would triumph over your difficulties. * * I bade you go on to Vienna, to have a brave heart, and do all you could for the exhibitors. * * * * Now how have you repaid me? You say you have been to me "true as steel," and have time and again expressed for me the most extravagant attachment. * * * * * * * *

Let us see how you have proven your regard. When you reached Vienna you informed Mr. McElrath that I had told you "to go right ahead and act as a Commissioner, as if you had not been suspended," thus charging me with direct disobedience to the orders of the State Department.

You stated you had never done a thing except by my orders.

You threatened to more than one person that if you were to fall, "you would drag down the whole Commission with you;" and to one, at least, that "if you were disgraced you intended to fall in good company, for General Van Buren should fall with you." When I learned that you had borrowed money from Boehm & Wiehl, I enquired of you if it were true, and you totally denied it; and when McElrath tried to persuade me you had done so, I affirmed it was untrue, because you had denied it.

Afterwards, when it was positively stated that you had obtained $1,000 of B. & W., * * you said to me you would explain that when you met those gentlemen face to face before Mr. Jay. A week afterwards you did so meet them, and I was astounded to learn that you had there acknowledged the receipt of the money and they had sworn to it. I afterwards learned, from Hitzel, that you had also received $500 from Mr. Dennison ; and a day or so since I was informed you had demanded and received $1,000 from the publisher of the catalogue. * * * * I have several times asked you why you did not go and finish your testimony, and have told you that if you had nothing to say against me your staying away would do me more harm than good, but your invariable answer has been, as before—a refusal. I have then said to you not to go there at all. In this connection, and no other, have I ever advised you not to go to the embassy, and you know it. * * * *

I now learn that you went to the Special Commission and testified that * * * I knew of your obtaining the $1,000 from B. & W. which you had once denied receiving at all, and afterwards said to me you would explain in their presence. You said I had taken Stiasney out of the way in order that you might get the money without his knowing it, when you know, as well as you know that you live, that I never dreamed of your having obtained this money from B. & W. * * * * * Having nothing to conceal I stated fully and clearly, in my first statement before the Special Commission, all I knew about these transactions, and you said to me that what I had stated was the truth, and you would testify to the same thing.

This is the way in which you have proved yourself "true as steel." Much of it has come to me within a few days. *
* * * * Now, in reference to money matters. How you dare, under any advice, retain Government monies committed to your keeping for a special purpose I cannot conceive! Your orders were to bring that money to me in Vienna. It is not yours in any sense. You were simply its custodian. It was drawn upon a requisition, stating precisely its uses, and is charged to me. It cannot legally be used for any other purposes than those stated in the requisition, and I warn you that your attempt to convert it to your own use will result disastrously. You are taking the very course to justify the Government in its treatment of you.

I would not have had my faith in you shattered for ten times the money involved. You will now probably do me every possible injury, if there is anything more you can do.

Let me say to you that I deprecate no hostility and ask no favors. There is no kindness I have not shown you. You now repay me in the way of the world, and confirm my determination to trust man no more.

After the receipt of this letter by Mayer the latter informed me that certain statements made by him in his testimony, he was convinced, were erroneous. That upon examinations of papers he was satisfied he had mistaken dates which made portions of his evidence incorrect, and that he had told or written to Mr. Jay not to use it on that account. He again stated that he knew nothing whatever to my injury, again expressed his undying attachment for me, and then, for the first time, admitted the receipt of the $1,000 from Boehm & Wiehl, which he had theretofore strenuously denied, in these words: "General, I did receive that money. I

got $500 when you were in Washington, and $500 at
another time." Had his testimony all been read to me,.
these facts would have appeared upon the record. As
to Mr. Stiasney's testimony, could I have been present
when it was given, I should have proven by him that it
was my daily custom to leave the lunch or dinner table
as soon as I had finished, and hurry to my business,
sometimes taking him, sometimes Mayer, sometimes going alone.

Upon my asking him in Vienna if this was not so, he
admitted that it was ; and to my further enquiry how it
was he could remember that "I called him away" on
the particular day mentioned in his evidence, he said he
was " made to remember," or words to that effect.

Mr. Wiehl, in his testimony, tells very plainly how he
came to form the impression that I had taken Stiasney
away on that occasion. He says "Mayer or some one
made a remark to that effect."

CHARGES.

The first charges of Mr. Jay were that there was evidence of " *gross corruption* in the commission in the sale
of concessions for bars and restaurants."

These charges I denounced as *foul and false.* I repeat
that statement and refer to the evidence as my justifica-
tion. His next allegations were that it was clearly shown
by my " admissions," and by the evidence, that I " had
taken money from the grantees of bars and restaurants."
I respectfully insist there is no such admission or evidence upon the record ; but on the contrary, there is my
explicit denial again and again repeated. And I submit,
also, that had the Government had that *evidence* before
them, instead of Messrs. Jay and McElrath's report of

its character, the removal and disgrace of my Commission could never have taken place.

Again I beg to call your attention to the fact that the telegrams of the Honorable Secretary of State to Mr. Jay under dates of April 26th and 28th in which he evidences his desire that myself and my associates should receive fair treatment, and that I should not be excluded from the opening ceremonies on the first of May, were kept carefully concealed from me by Mr. Jay, while he assured my friends that his task was a very hard and unpleasant one, for " General Van Buren was an old friend of his,"—thus seeking to make it appear that he was the unwilling instrument of the State Department in carrying out its harsh decrees.

Certainly neither the interests nor reputation of our Government required such a system of concealment, fraud, secret examinations, withholding and garbling evidence and general unfairness ; and I am confident it will, when fully understood, meet the condemnation of the Secretary to whom I wish here to acknowledge my obligations for many acts of courtesy and kindness, and especially for his effort to arrest the injustice done myself and my commission, which I have learned, for the first time, on reading this volume.

DELAYS IN MAKING REPORT.

Mr. Jay, in his dispatches of April 28th and 30th says, that no restoration of a commissioner should take place until the President could review all the facts and the testimony. Let it be remarked that the " investigation," so called, never closed until the 5th of July of this year, and then only upon the peremptory demand of the Depart-

ment of State; and not until this demand was thrice
repeated did he cease writing his final report which did
not reach Washington until the 23d day of July. As an
excuse for this delay, he reported to the Government
that the examination was prolonged at the "request of
the accused." By reference to the record it will be found
that it was the evident intention of Messrs. Jay and Mc-
Elrath that I should know nothing of the testimony and
have no opportunity of explanation, and that the investigation should not close until it was too late for any
action of the President in connection with the Exhibition.

I demanded, shortly after, the opening of their inquisi-
tion to be present at its sittings. In answer to this
I was called to give evidence, and informed by them, in
writing, that if any testimony should be thereafter given
which they should " deem affected the rights, interests or
honor of the American People, or of American Exhibitors, or that justice to General Van Buren himself should
demand," it should be submitted to me for such comment or explanation as I saw fit to give. (p. 215).

I received no sign, however, from the "Special Commission," and at last, moved by public rumor, I demanded again to be called before them for examination. That
examination took place on the 16th of May, and no further excuse has been offered for not closing the testimony.

The mass of evidence taken afterwards has no connection with the charges made by Mr. Jay.

Is it not a fair inference that they feared to submit to
the Government the flimsy proofs upon which they had
based their telegrams ? It is not true that I took money
from the grantees of bars and restaurants. I permitted

General Mayer to loan to me $500 for Commission expenses, which he had borrowed upon the voluntary offer of a man who had been granted a permit for a restaurant. That this loan from Hitzel might have been unwise is possible ; that it was corrupt or fraudulent, or in any way intended to affect his concession is false, and so conclusively shown to be by the testimony. That it was an " irregularity " demanding the disapproval and condemnation of the Government, I cannot conceive.

Reference to the testimony will show that the great mass of it had no relevancy to the matters committed to the Investigating Committee, and that none of it supports the telegrams of Mr. Jay, or the scandalous suggestions, insinuations and conclusions of his report. There is not a word in the evidence of any witness that charges me with the receipt of money except from General Mayer. That I believed that the two sums so received by me came from the parties named, was never for a moment denied or concealed, but that it was ever received by me in the spirit or with the motives indicated by Mr. Jay, is without warrant in the evidence, and his statements, therefore, in the telegrams of the 28th and 29th of April, signed by Messrs. Jay and McElrath, that the taking of money from the grantees of bars and restaurants had been admitted by me and proven by the evidence, were untrue in every essential particular.

My misfortune in this connection, is that Messrs. Jay and McElrath are shielded by their official positions from legal retribution ; and I am therefore compelled to expose their duplicity in my communications to you and to look to you for justice.

Before proceeding to analyze the report, I beg to

refer briefly to the character of the witnesses upon whose evidence it is chiefly based.

Mr. Henry L. Jewett, who appears to have been Mr. Jay's chief reliance in framing his charges, and who acted as his confidential friend and advisor, I learn was formerly connected with the collection of U. S. revenues at Brooklyn, N. Y.

His reputation there is not enviable, as I will show if *opportunity offers. And that reputation has not been improved at Vienna.

His motive in serving Mr. Jay was simply to prevent his former partner, whom he had swindled out of his permit, from obtaining any place on the Exhibition grounds.

In gratitude for his services, Mr. Jay recommends him to the gracious protection of the Government, (p. 548) but unfortunately for the harmony of this understanding, the recommendatien had scarcely been received at Washington before news came that Jewett had absconded from Vienna, owing a very large amount of money, and leaving his employees in a state of destitution. Mr. Jay's opinion as to the "explosion of this great scandal at Vienna" would prove interesting reading.

Mr. James, who was strongly recommended to me by Mr. Jay for Chief Engineer, and who was appointed an Assistant Commissioner, was chiefly useful in carrying rumors and reports of restaurant and bar-room conversations to the embassy (p. 100). Who this young man is, I have briefly stated in my letter to the Department (p. 136). His services in the commission consisted in spying and reporting for Mr. Jay, and in making a contract for roofing and flooring the court yard, which was freely denounced in Vienna as a fraud, and the price sworn to, to have been double what it should have been.

It was publicly charged in Vienna that James received a large per centage on this contract. The examination of this charge by Messrs. Jay and McElrath I submit was a farce, and the impropriety of their sitting in judgment upon it must be manifest. James was the confidant of Jay, and Mr. McElrath had himself signed the contract which was the subject of examination. Let it be remembered that I refused to make a payment on this contract; that I was removed from the commission, and the contract satisfied by Mr. Jay.

Mr. Stillman, the third of this interesting trio, was employed conjointly with James in reporting street and bar room gossip at the embassy, and in reflecting the views of Mr. Jay in scurrilous letters to The New York Tribune.

His performances as Consul in Crete are notorious. He has resided in England for some 17 years; entertains an inveterate hatred against everything American, and "is ready for a job." In what coin Mr. Jay paid for his services I don't stop to enquire, but only know that his intimacy at the embassy was the subject of much comment in Vienna.

These three "nobiles fratres" were the especial friends and intimates of Mr. Jay, and their information, advice and assistance he has acknowledged in his dispatches and report.

General Mayer, who was denounced by Mr. Jay as corrupt and unworthy, and as guilty, in his estimation, of the far worse crime of having been born on Austrian soil, of untitled parents, and perhaps of belonging to the Jewish faith, is held to be a good enough witness to condemn me. To the influences which induced General Mayer's testimony and its character, I have referred in another part of this communication. That he ever showed me a letter, which I forbid his publishing in the Vienna papers, as detailed by Stillman, is unequivocally false.

THE REPORT.

The evident unfairness of the report; its character as a special pleading; its labored attempts to twist and torture the testimony to my discredit; its imputations of unworthy motives for the most upright acts, and its general tone of malignity, I should suppose would stamp it with you as unworthy of consideration; but as it forms part of the record, I propose briefly to analyze it.

After opening with an announcement of the exceeding fairness of the examination, like the label of a patent medicine, this document states that the " rumors investigated related chiefly to charges of jobbing and corruption connected with the issue of permits in New York; and next to charges of careless and inefficient management."

Mr. Jay's telegrams and letters which led to the creation of his commission charged " corruption " distinctly, and this charge is repeated in his report of the 22d of April, (p. 132.)

In reply and in reference to this charge and this only was the examining tribunal commissioned, in these words:

" By order of the President, you and Thomas McElrath are appointed a special commission, with power to supervise the whole Commission to Vienna. You will examine and report fully, and are hereby authorized to suspend temporarily any person or persons appointed prior to 20th of March last, reporting the facts and the grounds of suspension."

What were these men ordered to "examine and report fully" if not the charges and rumors reported by Mr. Jay? I do not believe it was ever contemplated by the Government that the investigation was to extend over months and go into the entire workings of the Commission, and the private, public and family history and pedigree of each Commissioner.

It is evident from the order of the State Department above referred to, from the various telegrams to Mr. Jay demanding speedy examination and report, and the repeated orders to him to close the investigation and forward the papers to Washington, that the expectation of the Government was that the facts would be quickly gathered and laid before the President for his action.

I submit that by his failure to comply with these wishes of the Department, so often repeated, Mr. Jay has shown his motives to have been personal and not patriotic.

LOAN FROM HITZEL.

After reciting, with much circumlocution, the borrowing by Mayer from Hitzel of $500 and its subsequent use by me for expenses of the Commission, which was related fully to Mr. Jay at my first interview with him after my arrival in Vienna, and repeated in my formal evidence, the report goes on to say (p. 466):

"Although Mayer appears in this and other cases to have accepted and acted upon the view suggested by General Van Buren, to an extent of which Gen. V. B. himself declares he had no idea, Mr. Mayer's remark to Mr. Boehm on his arrival at Vienna, that there was trouble ahead, seemed to intimate that while he had practically adopted General Van Buren's advice, he was still doubtful either of its moral soundness or of its approval by the American people."

Were I not dealing with such a high dignitary as the American Minister to Austria, I should characterize this as contemptible pettifogging.

Nowhere does it appear that I gave advice to Mayer to get money, and his statement to Boehm that there "was trouble ahead," after he (Mayer) had been suspended by the procurement of Mr. Jay, was as much an indication of his "doubts as to the moral soundness" of his acts as it was of his belief in Mr. Jay's patriotism and sense.

The suggestion that accepting a loan from Hitzel could not be like that from a bank, because Hitzel was not a capitalist, is worthy the profound minds from which it eminated.

Mayer's statement that Stiasney and himself did not think Hitzel a proper person to come to Vienna, is directly contradicted by Mayer's own testimony, (p. 219) when he says:

"Knowing him (Hitzel) to be a *sober*, good man, [I told him] if General Van Buren was inclined to give him such permission [to erect a restaurant] I would speak a good word for it. I mentioned the subject to General Van Buren. Gen. V. B. at that time, however, had some conversation with a restaurateur named Cable and paid no attention to Hitzel until he found some objection on Cable's part to going."

Mr. Jay makes no reference to this, but goes on to state that the manner of Hitzel's payment hardly sustains the parallel between himself and a banker, inasmuch as Mayer says "the money was handed to him in small sums, on different occasions."

I only refer to this profound argument in order to show how it ignores the evidence and seeks to convey an entirely false idea of the facts.

First—Jewett (on page 171) says : "My impression is, the *first* check was for $500, drawn by Henry Schwaz, 306 Broadway;" and Hitzel swears (p. 275) : "I had given Mayer ($1,000), in two sums—a check for $500 of Henry Schwaz, and the rest ($500), which was paid in three checks, he paid back."

No word of Mayer's evidence to the contrary was ever read or shown to me, nor was I asked the question as to the shape in which this loan was made.

"But," says this ingenious accuser, prosecutor and judge, "the dependence of Hitzel upon Van Buren is shown by the testimony of the latter, 'that he told Hitzel, as he had told the others, that their places should be under strict police surveillance.'" (p. 468.)

Can anything be clearer? Is not corruption plainly proven in this extraordinary conduct of the Commissioner, in which he expresses his determination to see that no disorderly acts should be tolerated in any of these places ?

The statement of Mayer to which the report alludes, (p. 469) that the loan by Hitzel of $500 was in accordance with a former conversation by me with Hitzel, in his presence, was never shown to me by Mr. Jay, is utterly untrue, and is expressly contradicted by Hitzel (p. 276) when he says, "I never spoke to General Van Buren on the matter."

To the page of special pleading, (472) in which Mr. Jay exhausts his indignant virtue in denouncing a loan

or other receipt of money from Hitzel, I have to reply
that the " dignity and honor " of the Commission was
not assailed by Hitzel, nor was it in his power to do so.
It was left for Mr. Jay and his special favorite, the restaurateur and bar-keeper, Jewett, to make this assault
and bring disgrace upon the American name, not through
anything done by the Commission, but by the inexcusa-
ble conduct of the American Minister.

EXCUSE GIVEN BY MR. JAY.

In this connection I beg to call your attention to the
excuse given by Mr. Jay for his interference with my
commission, and the struggle on the part of Messrs. Jay
and Jewett to justify that interference afterwards. Says
Mr. Jay, (p. 92) " Conscious that such a scandal, *if ex-
ploded in Vienna*, amid an assemblage of the nations,
would bring upon the Administration and the country a
reproach more world-wide than any produced by local
corruptions at home, &c., &c., I did not hesitate, &c., &c."
On page 97 will be found a record of his efforts to prevent " the explosion " he so much deprecates. And the
striking contrast of the conduct of himself and his
friend Jewett upon the one side, and the plain common
sense of Mr. Wiehl upon the other, does not redound to
Mr. Jay's credit. Jewett, at the suggestion of James, it
seems, had established his intimacy with Mr. Jay, and
had persuaded Mr. Weihl to accompany him to the
Embassy, (p. 97.) When there Mr. Jay eagerly seized
his pen, " and," he says, " I intimated to Mr. Jewett
that I was ready to make a note of the conversation.
As he was beginning, Mr. Wiehl said, ' Stop a moment ;
I don't think I am ready to say anything to-day, at all
events, without consulting my partner. *It will stir up a
great row, and perhaps it had better be left alone.* Mayer

has done very wrong, but I don't like to put a gentleman in a false position.' "

I submit to you, Mr. Secretary, did not Wiehl, in these simple sentences, express your sentiments and those of the American people universally, and justify the confidence I had placed in him as a decent and honorable man? *Had my Commission been guilty of all that Mr. Jay charged, multiplied a hundred fold, was it his business to spread it out before the gathered world at Vienna, and fill with its details the newspapers of every nation? Was it not his duty, on the contrary, as the American Minister, to hush up the scandal, to keep the name and honor of his country untarnished, to labor for the success of the American Department of the Exhibition, and after its close to present his charges and proofs to the Government, and have the investigation at home?*

Mr. Jewett, however, with the approving smiles of Mr. Jay, replied to this remonstrance from Mr. Wiehl, that he wanted " to take the lead in exposing the scandal," and desired him (Wiehl) to join in the proceeding. " Mr. Wiehl replied, he must consult his partner."

Says Mr. Jay, " You may come, if you please, to-morrow, at half past eleven," etc., and then adds, " As they were going, I recalled Mr. Jewett, and said that perhaps he had better let me know what Messrs. Boehm & Wiehl resolved to do," or, in other words, " *Try and get Wiehl to testify, and we will manage to break up the commission yet.*"

The next day, Mr. Jay says, (p. 100) " I wrote you yesterday of an interview with Mr. Jewett and Mr. Wiehl. This morning Mr. Wiehl came alone, and said that he and his partner had resolved not to say anything about their treatment by Mr. Mayer. Mr. Jewett

might do as he pleased, *but they proposed to go on quietly.*"
"If they were required to say what passed, they would
tell the truth, *but they did not wish to make a disturbance,*"
etc.

Ah! but Messrs. Jay and Jewett did *not* wish things
to "go on quietly." They *did* want "a disturbance,"
and so they forced matters on until Mr. Wiehl supposed
himself obliged to give his evidence, which evidence, as
I shall show, has been garbled and misquoted by Mr.
Jay in his report.

MONEY NOT CREDITED.

"The money, although alleged to have been paid to
them officially, as Commissioners, was never credited to
the Commission," says the report. So far as I had
knowledge of any money transactions, the one was a
personal loan, and the other a subscription to be returned under certain circumstances. Had the subscription been used, it would have appeared on the record, as
ordered by me. It was not used, but returned. These
facts are repeatedly sworn to by every witness who had
knowledge of the transaction.

THE THIRD THOUSAND DOLLARS.

I wish now to call the attention of the Government
particularly to that portion of the report commencing on
page 480, in reference to what is called "the *third thousand dollars,*" which I charge as a deliberate misstate-
ment of the testimony, amounting almost to forgery.

There is no mention made in any part of the evidence
of Boehm & Wiehl or Mayer, of a "third thousand dollars."

Boehm says (p. 181), "The first $1,000 was a subscrip-
tion to the School House. The second, Mayer said he
would pay back when he came to Vienna"; and again

(p. 182) " *Two thousand dollars is all that has been paid by the firm of Boehm & Wiehl. No more has been asked for from them.*"

Mr. Wiehl, from whose evidence a quotation is made in this report, to justify its shocking perversion of facts, distinctly states, in that very evidence (p. 216), " While Mr. Boehm may have said," (referring to Jewett's reports), " that it cost us $3,000, *only $2,000 was paid the Commission, as stated.* The other $1,000 was paid to my lawyer, and had no connection with the Commission. I do not know of any other sum being paid to the Commission."

What respect can be paid to the allegations and arguments of men who, with these facts before them, can report to the Government exactly the contrary, and what shall be said of an American Minister who can prostitute his official name to such base uses?

Another unfounded statement appears in this report, on page 490, where it is written that a personal letter from myself to Mr. James, " dated at sea, March 23," contains a reference to " General Mayer's suspension." It is only necessary to remember that I had no knowledge of General Mayer's suspension until after I had reached Liverpool, to see that no such reference could have been made in that letter.

I submit that meddling with my private letters by Messrs. Jay and McElrath, was a high handed outrage at which most men would have hesitated ; but I shall ask *you* to characterize the act of suppressing the letter and misquoting its contents.

My statements in that letter were in reference to correspondence and conversations with you upon the subject of Mr. Jay's latest communications previous to my leaving New York. The fact that James carried this and all my letters to Mr. Jay I did not then know. It shows their relation to each other, and, I submit, justifies my assertions upon that subject.

While upon this topic, I venture to quote a few lines from a letter dated also " at sea," but addressed by me to Mr. Jay, to which he makes no reference.

I say, " During this long time of working and waiting, you and I have been carrying on what appeared to be a friendly correspondence. You have given me your views upon the proper conduct of the Commission, have suggested various ways of working up enthusiasm and procuring articles for exhibition, and have laid out programmes for me of a character requiring a vast amount of funds and the support of a vast number of men.

" I read your letters with every respect, but have ignored your programmes, for the reason that everything of value in them I had tried long before, so far as my means and the circumstances would permit. Your letters to me I held as personal and confidential, and I fully believed you were treating mine in the same manner. My letters were intended to be friendly conferences with one who I thought had given me his sympathy in my undertaking.

" You may, perhaps, then imagine my feelings, when I ascertained that while I was thus writing private, confidential, friendly letters to you, and receiving what appeared to be the same in reply, you were forwarding to the Department of State special despatches upon the subject of those letters, as well as private telegrams and letters to Mr. Fish, in which every expression of my fears, wrung from an overburdened body and mind, that the delays in Congress, and the general apathy, might yet render all my toil and expenditures valueless, was made to appear as evidence of my incapacity, or something worse.

" Not content even with this, you have charged that my only letters to Baron Schwarz Senborn were complaints as to bars and restaurants ; and, finally, your efforts have culminated in accusations of corruption and fraud.

" Now, I am not going to place myself on the defensive in any of these matters, nor do I feel called upon to make explanations to *you*. I will simply say that my correspondence with Baron Schwarz has been throughout of a satisfactory character, and that you are in possession of very little knowledge concerning it ; and that, when I reach Vienna, I shall endeavor to understand and expose the cowardly character of all assaults upon my honor, in whatever quarter they may have originated.

" In the meantime, I can only express my surprise and regret at the course you have seen fit to pursue."

The use of this private letter might have saved the necessity of appropriating and misquoting that to James. Its contents, however, will sufficiently explain why no use was made of it.

" His programmes sound like the proclamation of a Chinese emperor," I had said in another letter to James, which had been immediately carried to Mr. Jay, and served to inflame the latter's zeal in the " service of his country."

CHARACTER OF THE AMERICAN DEPARTMENT.

On page 506 of the report, begins a long criticism upon the character of the American department of the Exhibition, and of my correspondence and representations upon the subject. This piece of special pleading seems to me an impertinence not warranted by the authority under which the Special Commission was acting, or the facts and circumstances to which it refers.

To undertake to belittle my labors and misrepresent my situation, seems to have been a favorite pastime of Mr. Jay's, from the time of my appointment.

I shall be able to show, by evidence that cannot be questioned, the faithful and disinterested character of my efforts, the difficulties with which I had to contend, the obstacles I overcame, and the success which attended my work.

Mr. Jay takes exceptions to my remark that I would have been justified in not advancing money or devoting my entire time and exertions in procuring an exhibition from the United States, until after an appropriation by Congress. The importance and value of the services of Mr. Jay are doubtless very great. His triumphs as a diplomat, are they not written in the archives of the State Department, and his exalted reputation as the most successful representative of democratic-republican institutions in all Europe, does it not add lustre to our Government? He receives for all this expenditure of profundity, elegance and politeness the sum of $12,500, in gold, yearly, in addition to some thousands for an outfit.

Besides he has the diplomatic privilege of entering, free of duty, certain articles for his household; for an over-exercise of which privilege, I am told, he has been taken to task by the Austrian Government.

I fail to discover in these facts evidence of that disinterestedness and selfsacrifice which Mr. Jay so eloquently commends. Whatever *my* theory of the obligations of *my* official position, *I* did labor early and late, without reward and at my own expense, with no certainty of being reimbursed a dollar.

And here let me remark that the amount of that outlay is not to be measured by the accounts rendered, by me, to the Government. The expenses to which I was subjected on account of my position, exhausted my entire income, and have left me burdened with debt.

So far as I have been able to ascertain, I was the only Commissioner, from any nation, who was obliged to dance attendance at the seat of Government, begging an appropriation of money to secure an exhibition of his country's products. Every other government made its appropriation without solicitation from the Commissioner, and at a time when it could be used to the greatest advantage.

I think it cannot be denied that, without my exertions, no appropriation would have been secured from Congress ; and that, without that appropriation, no exhibition would have been possible from this country. I repeat that until that appropriation was made, I would have been fully justified in not exhausting my time and means to secure such exhibition.

As Commissioner from the United States, I could have performed the duty of visiting the Exhibition, and reporting to my Government my observations and such facts as were of value concerning it. Waiting, as I did, upon Congress from week to week, now hoping, now despairing, it is not to be wondered at that my letters reflected these different feelings. I was interested and anxious in my work, and no effort was spared in my office to make our department a success—as no effort

was afterward spared by the Honorable John Jay and
his associates to depreciate and ruin it.

I deny that in any fair sense our Exhibition was a
failure. The want of large and showy cases in which to
exhibit the goods, made it less attractive to the eye than
were the other departments ; but in the character of the
materials, it was a success. This is proven by the number of awards granted to exhibitors, and will, I am certain, be fully demonstrated when the final report of the
Commission is received. The attempt to convict me of
misrepresentation as to the number of applications from
exhibitors, seems to be based upon letters written by me
to several gentlemen, members of Congress and others.

I have only to say that, while it is possible I may
have used expressions in those letters somewhat exag-
gerated, it remains true that more applications were received and more granted than we then had space at our
command, and to add that *this* inquiry also is without
the scope of Mr. Jay's authority. Many of the permits
were not used on account of the delays in the appropriation, and others on account of the scandal created by
Mr. Jay. He asserted in one of his letters that contributions other than those sent by me were secured. I
challenge proof of this statement, which I insist is without the least foundation in fact. What was sent from
this country was so sent by the devoted toil of myself
and my associates.

SPACE.

This brings me to consider the question of space.
From the number of applications, it appeared absolutely
necessary to so arrange the uncovered portion of our
space *in* the Exhibition building as to fit it for use.
Upon this subject I corresponded with Mr. Jay and

Assistant Commissioner James, and instructed the latter to have the work done as speedily and cheaply as possible. His estimates forwarded to me increased with every mail, and seemed so extravagant and so disproportioned to the amount and character of the work and materials required, that I did not hesitate to express my opinion to that effect. This was explained in his letters by charging it upon the piling and heavy side walls, rendered necessary, as it was said, by the character of the ground and weight of the superstructure. My distance from Vienna made me dependent upon the judgment of my assistants on the spot. Mr. McElrath reached Vienna in time to examine the contract prepared by Mr. James for this work, and to execute it for the Commission. This contract was for $30,000 of our money in gold, papable in French coin, upon which there was a large premium, for a structure which proved to consist of *floor and roof alone, without either piles or side walls,— the whole to revert to the contractors at the close of the Exhibition.* So that, in fact, the price paid was for the mere rental of the building for six months, while the rental of the space inside was again paid by exhibitors.

In view of all these facts it is not to be wondered at. that witnesses gave it as their opinion that the structure should not have cost one half the amount, and that the the rumor was current in Vienna that the contract was. tainted with corruption.

Under the circumstances, I refused to make a third payment upon the contract, two having been made. before my arrival. I was removed, and the contract immediately satisfied by Mr. Jay. *Had there been other covered space in the main building, which could have been pro-*

cured for our uses, it would have avoided any portion of this large expenditure.

If it was ever within the scope of Mr. Jay's duty to see to this business, clearly this was the time to exercise that suave wisdom and diplomatic skill for which he is distinguished. I do not find, however, from the record, that he took any steps whatever to secure such additional space. On the contrary, he approved the contract for covering the court yard, and made haste to pay the large sum named in it.

After this was done, however, Mr. Jay suddenly awakened to the idea of securing more space, and when I reached Vienna he was radiant with triumph. According to his own statements he had accomplished a great work. He had bombarded the Chief of the Austrian Commission, the British Minister and Commission, and the Commissioners from South America, with his unanswerable and almost unending diplomatic notes, and had finally succeeded in "backing England down from a portion of the space occupied by her," (to use his own words,) and secured one half the entire transept of South America for our use.

The British Minister declined any responsibility, it being reserved for the Minister from the U. S. to interfere with the Commission from his country.

Had Mr. Jay, with my approval, secured this additional space before covering the court yard, it would have obviated the necessitity of such covering. As it was, I cannot understand by what authority he acted. Observe that it was done without consultation with the Commission, and just previous to the opening of the Exhibition. He had not secured an article to put in this space, and as *I* had no conception it was to be procured, I had taken no steps to fill it.

Had not this unwarranted interference taken place, or had he informed the Commission of his intentions in time, all our room in the Exhibition buildings would have been creditably filled. As it was he found himself with a large additional space on hand, to be paid for by the Government, and not an exhibitor to occupy it. After my removal, however, Mr. Jay, as supreme controller of our department, caused that new space to be first filled from the objects I had collected, leaving, of course, vacancies in our original transept and court yard. And these very vacancies, thus created, he makes the subject of censure in his report.

ADVISORY COMMITTEE.

I have heretofore remarked as to the quality of the articles exhibited from this country, which commended them to the approval of the juries and the admiration of the Emperors of Germany and Austria and the members of their respective courts. And now I refer for a moment to the criticism passed upon me for not leaving the selection of these articles entirely to the Advisory Committee, in New York. The Advisory Committee was composed of gentlemen selected by me, whose action was entirely voluntary. I respectfully contend that if this Committee had never been called upon to act, such omission on my part is not properly the subject of complaint from Mr. Jay, or from any parties except the gentlemen composing the Committee. But the fact is that I made every possible exertion to secure the co-operation of the different branches of the Advisory Committee, and it was only when most of these failed to act, and the shortness o time permitted no alternative, that I assumed the unpleasant task myself.

It is charged by Messrs. Jay and McElrath that I neglected to send to Vienna, weeks before my arrival the full assignments of space in our department, while at the same time I am taken to task for not referring all this to the Advisory Committee. The truth is, the time for doing the work necessary for so large an undertaking was entirely too limited. Everything possible was done by myself and my associates. Mr. McElrath was one of the Assistant Commissioners; I look in vain, however, for evidences of his activity in behalf of the Exhibition. While we were laboring without cessation, he was enjoying the leisure and luxury of a sojourn in Italy, until he came to Vienna to conspire against the head of the Commission and his associates, and complacently accept the honors due them.

LEAVING BUSINESS WITH MAYER.

I am accused also of having, while in Washington, left the business of the Commission in the hands of General Mayer, when, in the opinion of Mr. Jay, I should not have troubled myself by seeking an appropriation from Congress, but should have accepted the offers of those who were willing to contribute to the expenses of the Commission. He says I could easily have secured commissioners of such wealth and standing as to have commanded from them a generous contribution. (p. 515.) In England, he adds, a large amount was given by private citizens, "one of the Commission himself contributing 10,000 pounds." This was denied to me by members of the British Commission, the fact being that what was contributed was for special objects. But suppose I had accepted such contributions, would not Mr. Jay have been the first to condemn my action. The chief burden of his complaint now is that I permitted a person even to loan a small sum to the Commission, or any member of it, or to subscribe to the expenses of erecting a school house or other building.

It has sometimes occurred to me to enquire why it is that Mr. Jay did not follow the example of the English Gentleman he so approvingly quotes, and forward to the Commission his contribution of ten thousand pounds. Thus, by his works, he would have illustrated the value of his words. Instead of this, he sent me an urgent request, before the appropriation was made, to re-imburse him a few dollars he had unwittingly expended in the premises. After Mr. Jay had succeeded in securing my removal, he carried out his idea of appointing men of "wealth and standing." I submit to you whether the experiment was satisfactory. I know in his report he gives great credit to this Temporary Commission, but the facts scarcely sustain his eulogy, as I shall show when opportunity presents.

Suppose I had appointed these, or similar parties, to have assisted me at the outset : does any one believe I would have ever secured an exhibition ? I am told that they received the Emperor and his suite on the first of May, under the supervision of Mr. Jay, with infinite grace, and having thus secured the success of the Exhibition, they resigned the next day.

The course adopted by myself, with regard to my appointments and the appropriation, seemed to me the only proper one. In my absence, I was, of course, obliged to leave the office in the hands of a deputy. So far as my experience goes, every public officer does the same thing, Mr. Jay, not excepted. That Mr. Mayer did the entire work and bore the responsibility of the office, however, is simply absurd.

THE SCHOOL HOUSE.

As to my authority given to Col. Bridges to erect the school room, and of Mr. Philbrick's extended testimony upon the general subject, I have only to say that looking over my action in the premises, in view of all the facts and circumstances, I am of the opinion that my course was not only entirely justified, but is highly to be commended. Mr. Philbrick's statement (*not offer*,) that some patent structure could be put on board a ship in Boston harbor, in pieces, at a cost of $2,800 was of no sort of importance. Had such contract been made, the building, put up at Vienna, would have cost far more than the one erected. His promise that Boston would pay a portion of the expense was withdrawn, and I understand him to favor my action in the premises. At any rate, the responsibility belonged to me, and not to Mr. Philbrick. The school building was erected at the very lowest possible price. Its exhibition was a great success, as the reports will show, and if my Commission had not been interfered with, I believe no criticism would have been made upon my action or upon this part of the Exhibition.

WANT OF FRANKNESS.

I refer now to that part of the report that charges me with " want of frankness " in my correspondence with the State Department. (p. 540.) My letter to the Secretary which is thus commented on, and which appears on page 103, I affirm is true and frank in every particular. " Want of candor and frankness " is shown *not* in my letters, but in the misrepresentations and misquotations of this report. On page 542, will be found this language, referring to my letter: " Here was no intimation that Boehm & Wiehl were to have three establishments, two of which were being erected on the grounds, and that the third, General Van Buren had himself suggested to Baron Schwarz *should* be placed in the Rotunda of the Palace of Industry." And a little farther on they say: " For this deliberate misrepresentation of the truth accompanied with an expression of regret if the Department should disapprove of his establishment of one bar, the Special Commission find no apology." Now, either this " Special Commission " or myself is guilty of a "deliberate misrepresentation of the truth ;" I adopt their own polite and diplomatic phrase.

By a paragraph on page 543, it will be seen that the charge is repeated that I did not tell the truth in reference to the number of permits given by me for restaurants and bars. Now, if it be shown, from the evidence, that I never gave Boehm & Wiehl permission to erect *three places* for the sale of liquors ; and never did suggest to Baron Schwarz " that a bar *should* be erected in the rotunda," as stated by Mr. Jay, there will be no difficulty in deciding which of us is guilty of " deliberate misrepresentation of the truth." Reference to my letter to Baron Schwarz introducing Boehm & Wiehl, (p. 180) which Mr. Jay quotes, as the foundation of his charges, will show that no allusion whatever is made to any permission on my part to them, other than for the erection of " one pavilion ;" and the correspondence and evidence may be searched in vain to find a single reference, on my part, either to a permit for the erection of a " Wigwam," or that I had the least knowledge that the same was being erected. The *fact* is that I. never heard a word upon the subject until after my arrival in Vienna. As to the bar in the rotunda, my exact language is as follows : " If it should seem to you best to grant these parties an additional permit to erect a small bar in the rotunda of the Palace of Industry, *I have no objection* to its being done, and will have a supervision over it. Anything they undertake to do I feel perfectly assured will be well done."

In writing to the State Department, this sentence, in my letter to Boehm & Wiehl had escaped my memory, but I submit it is not " suggesting to Baaon Schwarz that a bar *should* be erected," as stated by Mr. Jay. It was given by me at the solicitation of Boehm & Wiehl as simply indicating that I would not oppose such permit if they could obtain it from 'Baron Schwarz. These then are the facts. I gave no permit to B. & W. to erect " three places for the sale of drinks," nor did I suggest that " a bar *should* be erected in the rotunda ;" but the statement in my letter to the Department that I had granted permits for the erection of " one pavilion for the sale of drinks," " and one restaurant," was the literal and exact truth, and the statements of Messrs. Jay and McElrath to the contrary are literal and exact " misrepresentations of the truth."

CHARACTER OF THE REPORT.

I am now about through with this report, in which Messrs. Jay and McElrath have exhausted their utmost ingenuity to convict me of some offense to justify their flaming telegrams and reports, and the disgrace brought upon our Government and people.

I repeat : The charge in their dispatches was that of " corruption," in the taking of money from the keepers of bars and restaurants, and their recommendation that the Commission be suspended upon the general charge of " irregularities," such " irregularities " being the "corruption" named. The answer of the Government was the suspension of the Commission "on account of the 'irregularities' referred to." My accusers and judges have diligently employed themselves for three months to get together something to justify or excuse their action in the premises, and would probably be still engaged in the same agreeable employment if not arrested by the positive command of the State Department. The result is before you, and I submit that with all their anxiety and all the power in their command, even in the microscope of their malice, they have failed to discover a single act which merits the disapproval of the Government.

If any error was committed by me in connection with bars or restaurants, it is needless to say, to those who know me, that such error was not the fruit of corruption. *I did what I thought was for the best, and submitted my action to the Government for its examination and approval or disapproval, avowing my readiness to abide by its orders.*

The behavior of Mr. Jay, however, throughout this whole affair, I submit, was contrary to that of a good citizen having the fair fame of his country at heart, and particularly unbecoming in a representative of our Government in a foreign country, whose first duty it was to shield the honor of the Republic and protect his countrymen from oppression.

I now ask, upon this whole matter, the judgment and action of the Government. It is said that officers having no fixed tenure of office may be removed without cause assigned Without stopping to question this assumption, it is sufficient to say that in *this* case *charges were made* by Mr. Jay, and an extraordinary tribunal, whose conduct is without precedent in our history, labored for three months, in a foreign city, to establish them.

If these charges have not been sustained, I ask that my reputation may be vindicated by the Government, or that a thorough investigation may be had, before a committee of Congress, of everything connected with our Exhibition at Vienna from its inception to its close, under its four different commissions, with the details of its management and expenses, the character and services of the parties employed at Vienna, and also the conduct and motives of Messrs. Jay and McElrath in connection therewith, as well as of their qualifications to act as judges of my Commission.

ASSISTANT COMMISSIONERS.

I cannot close this communication without referring, for a moment, to the removal of those Assistant Commissioners, against whom even the malice of Mr. Jay could invent no charge. Nothing was imputed to them except that their appointment was due to me. Going to Vienna, having devoted months to their official duties, and bearing the commissions of their Government, they were suddenly thrust from their positions, and refused the least explanation or redress.

At the suggestion of the Government that Mr. Shultz should select his assistants from among these gentlemen, two of them were reappointed, one of whom was afterwards made chief of the Commission.

Mr. McMichael was re-instated, but refused to serve, and Dr. Ruppaner journeyed from Vienna to Washington and back to regain his position ; but it seems proper to enquire why the others were ignored while the services of some of them were eagerly sought and received by the new Commission! Messrs. Round and Gottheil performed most valuable labors at the Exhibition, and the important duties confided to the latter by the existing Commission have kept him at Vienna up to the present time.

It seems scarcely creditable that these men should have received only disgrace at the hands of their country's representative in Austria, while Mr. McElrath, who never did any service for the Commission, was loaded with praises and honors.

I have been accused of too much zeal in my own defence and that of my Commission.

Christian forbearance is a virtue so easily preached by those who have received no injury! But righteous indignation against such wrongs as we have been subjected to, I cannot think unbecoming in men conscious of their rectitude and who know their own rights.

For one, I desire most respectfully to say that I refuse to rest quietly under the assaults made upon my character until publicly vindicated.

This vindication is not necessary to my neighbors and friends, who nobly sustained me at the outset of the attack, and also after a careful reading of the evidence and report filed by Mr. Jay; nor to my acquaintances, who, with scarcely an exception, have hastened to express to me their entire confidence in my honor; nor to those who know Mr. Jay and are familiar with his character disposition and habits; nor to the Government, which announces it has made no charges accusing me "of any criminality or improper conduct;" but to that great public, here and abroad, before which my name has been for months held up to scorn and contempt, it is due that the truth should be fully exposed,

4

that it should be shown that I have not only been guilty of no wrong, but that I have rendered a service to the Government and people, and accomplished a work that should entitle me to approbation rather than censure—to rewards rather than reproaches.

I have the honor to be, Sir, with great respect,

Your obedient servant,

THOS. B. VAN BUREN.

P. S.—While the foregoing was being printed I have received the announcement of my nomination as Consul-General at Japan, which affords me the gratifying conviction that I still possess the confidence and regard of the Government, and am vindicated by its public act. I send this to you now in order that it may form a part of the record of the "Vienna Exhibition" on file in your Department.

www.ingramcontent.com/pod-product-compliance
Lightning Source LLC
Chambersburg PA
CBHW021429090426
42739CB00009B/1420